Original title:
Gleaming Gifts and Winter Whispers

Author: Tobias Winslow
ISBN HARDBACK: 978-9916-90-894-5
ISBN PAPERBACK: 978-9916-90-895-2

Glorious Chill with a Slice of Light

A snowman rolled up, oh what a sight,
With a carrot nose that’s not quite right,
He wobbles and jiggles, trying to dance,
Fumbling and falling, oh what a chance!

Hot cocoa spills on the frosty ground,
Marshmallows bob like a soft surround,
I sip and I slurp, hot chocolate delight,
As my friends all giggle, sharing their plight.

Tinsel and twinkle lights everywhere,
They tangle and twist, an absolute scare,
We pull and we tug, it's a tangled mess,
Laughter erupts, what a festive stress!

Frosty breath shows in the chilly air,
Snowflakes flutter without a care,
We slide on ice, oh what a thrill,
I’ll perfect this falling — it’s quite a skill!

The Courage of Small Flames in the Dark

In the corner, candles flicker,
A bug flew by, gave me a sticker.
Sighing softly, I made a wish,
For buttered popcorn, not a fish.

Tiny sparks in darkened rooms,
Fight the shadows, banish glooms.
With laughter shared, hearts feel light,
Even if the snacks take flight!

Soft Radiance Illuminating the Silence

A flashlight's beam upon my nose,
I trip on toys, oh dear, who knows?
In the quiet, giggles sprout,
As we wonder what life's about.

Under blankets, whispers soar,
Hot cocoa spills on the hardwood floor.
In this glow, we share our dreams,
And strategize our snack-filled schemes.

Nature’s Baubles Dressed in White

Snowflakes dancing, what a sight!
They land on snowmen, oh so bright.
With carrot noses and hats askew,
They wink at us — ‘We’re here for you!’

Icicles hang like candy canes,
Dripping slowly, on window panes.
As we sip our drinks and grin,
The warmth inside is where we win!

Charms of the Season's Glistening Touch

Ornaments jingle on the tree,
Cats pounce, oh what a jubilee!
With tinsel strewn like cats in play,
We laugh until the end of day.

Cookies crumbled on the floor,
Do you hear the puppy's roar?
With joy we gather, hearts are full,
In this chaos, life is a pull.

Shining Secrets of Winter's Nightfall

In the hush of the night's embrace,
Snowflakes dance with a silly grace.
Elves slip on ice with laughter bright,
Chasing shadows, a merry sight.

Hot cocoa spills, oh what a mess,
Mugs overflow, pure happiness.
While snowmen wear hats a tad askew,
They grin at the antics, just like we do.

Frosted Paths to Hidden Bounty

Sleds zoom fast, a frosty burst,
In the snowy hills, kids' laughter first.
A snowball fight breaks out with flair,
One poor chap's caught unaware!

Carrots for noses, the jokes unfold,
Snowmen's secrets, oh they're bold!
With candy canes found in every nook,
It's a winter tale right from a book.

Whispered Glories in the Winter's Heart

Twinkling lights like wishes made,
Under the stars, friendships displayed.
With mittens too big, a juggling act,
They drop the cookies, a tasty fact!

Pine trees dressed like fashion queens,
Laughter hides in the evergreen scenes.
When snowflakes fall as confetti bright,
Joy and chaos fill the night.

Radiant Trails on the Snowy Canvas

Footprints lead to a frozen lake,
Where ducks waddle like they're late.
Ice skates slip, a tumble here,
But giggles rise, oh what a cheer!

With berry pie cooling on a sill,
The aroma blends with the winter chill.
A cat leaps softly, to take a peek,
At snowy adventures, so unique.

Glittering Boughs Beneath Crystal Skies

Whirls of snow dance like clumsy pals,
Squirrels don tuxedos, all dressed in style.
The trees wear hats of frost and ice,
While birds play tag, oh, isn’t that nice?

Chilly winds sing a song off-key,
But who cares when there's hot cocoa with glee?
Snowmen gossip about the best hats,
Laughing at snowballs thrown by chubby cats.

Enchanted Flakes of Midnight Magic

Frosty flakes giggle as they twirl,
Landing on noses, causing a whirl.
Elves on stilts juggle icicles bright,
While reindeer toast marshmallows at night.

Snowflakes gossip, “Did you hear?”
One fell on a snowman, giving him cheer.
They whisper jokes, but they melt so fast,
Leaving behind puddles that make a splash.

Illuminated Paths Through Icy Woods

A raccoon in boots slips on a route,
While the owls hoot, "What's that all about?"
The trees in the woods sparkle and shine,
Pinecones drop gifts, all wrapped in twine.

With each crunch of snow, laughter peeks through,
A snowball flies, oh — who threw that? You?
The paths are lined with giggles and cheer,
As we dash through the woods, let's not shed a tear.

Whispered Blessings in the Frozen Air

Gusts of laughter take flight like kites,
While neighbors debate how to brave the bites.
In paper-thin houses, the rumors grow,
“Who stole the cookies?” we want to know!

Frosted windows hide giggling mates,
As we nibble away on the holiday plates.
Jingle bells ringing, echoing fun,
Winter's a laugh, when it’s all said and done.

Brilliant Snowflakes on a Silver Canvas

Snowflakes dance like tiny stars,
Creating chaos, giggles, and jars.
They land on noses, and hats askew,
Just blame it all on a sneaky gust too.

We build a man with a carrot nose,
His arms are made from two old toes.
He wobbles, giggles, then starts to sway,
And soon he's melting all our fun away.

Whispers of Frost on a Gentle Breeze

The wind sneezes, oh what a sound,
As frosty whispers swirl all around.
A snowman coughs, his hat falls off,
His snowy belly shakes like a scoff.

We chase our hats through fields of white,
With laughter echoing through the night.
Icicles dangle like shiny teeth,
Oh winter fun, you're a frosty wreath!

Illuminated Solitude in a Snowy Glade

In a snowy glade where the moonlight beams,
Critters plot with their candy dreams.
A squirrel in boots, a chipmunk in shades,
They dance on branches like acrobat parades.

Snowballs fly, a fluffy brigade,
While rabbit aces a jump off the jade.
Laughter erupts, echoing so bright,
As winter's whimsy stirs the night!

Soft Hues in the Cold Embrace of Night

Twinkling lights hang from every nook,
While hot cocoa bubbles in a festive cookbook.
Snowflakes play tricks on the roof's old edge,
As the cat dances near a frosty hedge.

With mittens slipping, we take a fall,
And land in a snowbank, oh what a call!
We are bundled, laughing, with no care in sight,
In this chilly wonderland of pure delight.

Frosty Whispers Beneath Winding Pines

In frosty air, the snowmen grin,
They trade their hats, let the fun begin!
With carrot noses, they start to dance,
Twirling ‘round in a snowy romance.

The trees all giggle, their branches sway,
As pinecone buddies join in the play.
A squirrel slips, but it’s all in cheer,
Who knew winter could bring such a year?

A Bounty of Light in the Quiet Woods.

The lanterns glow like mismatched socks,
Hiding treats in the old wooden box.
Raccoons wear scarves, looking so chic,
While rabbits chuckle and share a sneak peek.

The owls hoot loudly, they've lost their hats,
While frosty wind plays silly old chats.
Each twig is a story, a jolly delight,
In shimmering glimmers, they laugh at the night.

Shimmering Tokens of the Frost

Snowflakes giggle as they tumble down,
They tickle noses of folks in the town.
A penguin waddles with a penguin flair,
Dancing around, acting like he's rare.

With pockets stuffed full of snow and cheer,
Snowball fights break out, laughter we hear!
The frost teases toes with icy surprise,
Yet everyone grins with twinkles in eyes.

Secrets of the Silent Snow

The secrets we share in the hush of the night,
Are whispered by stars, oh what a sight!
Pine trees gossip of things that they saw,
As blankets of snow hide it all with a paw.

A deer in a scarf hops over the stream,
With friends in the woods, they plot and they scheme.
Chasing each other, they trip and they fall,
In the laughter of winter, there's magic for all.

Whispered Wishes in the Crystal Air

Amidst the snow, a squirrel leaps,
He hides his stash while giggling heaps.
A snowman sighs, his nose a carrot,
He dreams of summer, oh how to bear it.

Frosty breath escapes with delight,
While penguins strut in coats so tight.
A snowball fight ignites the cheer,
As laughter dances, winter's here!

Radiant Shadows of the Frosty Dawn

Morning light on frosted ground,
A cat chases shadows all around.
With every leap, she sneezes bright,
Cold air tickles, what a sight!

Elves with hats too large to wear,
Run in circles, with flair to spare.
Hot cocoa spills on chilly toes,
They giggle as the snowman grows!

Delicate Glimmers in the Deep Chill

Icicles hang like teeth of glee,
While gingerbread men dance with glee.
Whipped cream clouds float on mugs so wide,
The winter tales we can't abide.

Birds in hats try to sing sweet tunes,
But end up laughing at their loons.
Snowflakes twirl like ballerinas,
In a dizzy dance with hot marinas!

Songs of the Winter's Embrace

In a world of flurries, all is bright,
A snow cat prowls, seeking a bite.
Dressed in mittens, birds take flight,
Chasing cheeky dreams with all their might.

Snowmen chat with reindeer near,
Trading jokes that warm the sphere.
With every snicker, joy erupts,
In this frosty land where laughter cups!

Silent Sparkles in the Snow

The snowflakes danced like tiny clowns,
Making funny faces, wearing frowns.
They twirled and slipped with a silly cheer,
While penguins snickered—"What’s that you hear?"

A snowman lost his carrot nose,
Searching for it where the cold wind blows.
He peeked behind a frozen tree,
And yelled, "Darn it! Where can I be?"

Frosted Dreams of Solstice Eve

The stars looked down with a cheeky grin,
As squirrels practiced their acrobatic spin.
Tinsel wrapped around a porcupine,
He shrugged and said, "I look divine!"

The hot cocoa smirked in a cozy cup,
"Don't you dare go and spill me up!"
Frothy marshmallows giggled with glee,
As they pondered on who would brew the tea.

A Tapestry of Frost and Light

A kitten wrapped in a ball of yarn,
Gazed at the snow with a look of charm.
"Is that a snack or a fluffy foe?"
She pounced and tumbled, oh what a show!

The icicles laughed, draped down like hats,
As rabbits leaped by, making loud splats.
"Watch out!" they cried, skidding through frost,
In a race to treasure—never lost!

Shimmering Echoes of the North

The breeze told tales of a wise old moose,
Who wore a scarf made of colorful juice.
"One sip and I dance like a silly goat,"
He chuckled loud, spinning like a boat.

The Northern lights twinkled, turned upside down,
As a snowball fight broke across the town.
Laughter echoed, a symphonic spree,
In the land where giggles were always free.

Dazzling Moments in the Hushed White

Snowflakes drop like butter pats,
Lopsided snowmen wear funny hats.
I slipped on ice, did a dance,
The snowdog stared, as if to prance.

Hot cocoa spills on my warm mitts,
Marshmallows float, never fits.
Each snowy trail smells like my sock,
A cheeky elf watches from the clock.

Witty squirrels with their acorns dance,
While I try to catch them in a glance.
They toss their food, a playful game,
As if they plan to stake their claim.

Winter nights and frozen toes,
Giggles echo as laughter grows.
With jokes and warmth, this time's a thrill,
As snowflakes twirl, we laugh until.

Serene Glimmers Amidst Winter's Stillness

Icicles shine like shiny teeth,
Held by roofs in a snow-covered wreath.
A muffled giggle breaks the cold,
As snowball fights get funny and bold.

Fuzzy hats and mismatched mitts,
We stumble, laugh, fall with fits.
The wind whispers secrets of the chill,
While I chase the dog, up and downhill.

Chubby bunnies hop around,
Their fluffy tails bounce, joy unbound.
In a world so white, we forget our woes,
As snowflakes dance and tickle our nose.

Curling up by the fire's bright glow,
The cat jumps in, stealing the show.
With tales of snow and chilly cheer,
We laugh as we sip, our joy sincere.

Frost-kissed Memories Drenched in Light

Frosty mugs and chatter loud,
Silly slips bring giggles proud.
Beat-snowmen with noses of coal,
Look sideways, as if with a soul.

Snowdrifts high, they're fortresses now,
But I sneak in, with a silly bow.
A surprise attack from the neighbor's kid,
And soon enough, we all outbid.

Socks all mismatched, where did they go?
One’s on the cat, the other below.
We laugh at our blunders, oh what a sight,
As winter silliness feels just right.

Kick back and warm, with tales well-spun,
As stars twinkle down on our nightly fun.
With every sip of our cocoa delight,
This frosted world’s a pure delight.

Celestial Gifts Beneath the Starry Veil

Stars twinkle like winks in the night,
While we bundle up, all snug and tight.
A snowman wears a scarf that's bright,
With broccoli arms, what a silly sight!

On icy paths, there's mischief afoot,
I trip and fall, my socks all wet.
The dog pounces, it's time for a chase,
While the moon chuckles, making grace.

Chubby cheeks kiss the chilly air,
With laughter echoed everywhere.
As pine trees glow in twinkling light,
We build memories, hearts feeling light.

Homeward bound, we share our fate,
With stories and snacks on our dinner plate.
Through winter's charm, we find our glee,
Under this blanket, just you and me.

Warmth Frozen in a Winter's Caress

A penguin wore a hat, so neat,
In snowball fights, he can’t take a seat.
His flippers fling with comic grace,
As snowflakes dance all over the place.

The cocoa pots are full of cheer,
But marshmallows fly, oh dear, oh dear!
They bounce around like little mice,
In a mug so warm, it's silly and nice.

Where snowmen laugh with carrot noses,
And icy paths are a dance of poses.
With mittens stuck in snowdrifts deep,
They bungle about, frosty and cheap.

So let the cold bring joyful flights,
With laughter ringing through the nights.
Wrapped up warm in joy and glee,
In this frozen world, we're wild and free.

Shining Dreams Adrift in the Chill

The frost bites hard, but I can’t resist,
To sled down hills, oh what a twist!
Each bump sends me flying in pure delight,
Landing in snow with laughter so bright.

The hare wears boots quite out of style,
He trips and falls with a goofy smile.
While winter winds blow all around,
In this comical scene, joy is found.

Hot soup spills in a funny pot,
Twirl it once, and it's in a knot!
While snowflakes tickle and make us sneeze,
Our giggles echo through frosty trees.

So gather round, share stories and tales,
Of snowmen’s antics and wind’s howler wails.
This chilly season, though cold and stark,
Brings laughter and fun, lighting up the dark.

Icy Blossoms of the Winter's Bloom

In a garden where ice flowers grow,
A squirrel in shades puts on quite a show!
He slips and slides with grace so rare,
While trying to dance in the frosty air.

Snowflakes twirl on a cat's furry back,
As they plot to launch a mischievous attack.
But oh, they tumble and fall so slow,
A winter wonderland of giggles aglow.

Chilly pets in their cozy coats,
Chase after shadows and stoats on boats.
With fur all fluffed like cotton candy,
They pounce and roll, the scene is dandy!

So let snowy antics write their rhyme,
And echo through a playful time.
For in this frost, with humor so sweet,
We find our joy in every heartbeat.

Celestial Sparkles in the Quiet Night

Under the stars, a snowman sings,
With silly tunes and twinkling rings.
His carrot nose glows in a bright hue,
While the moonlight chuckles at this crew.

A penguin dreams of warm sunny sands,
But wakes to snow in frosty bands.
He waddles about, lost in a thought,
In his dreams, he's shared quite a lot!

The winter’s chill brings all sorts of fun,
From snowball fights under the sun.
As laughter mingles with starlit skies,
We find our joy in surprise-filled sighs.

So gather 'round with glee and light,
For the magic awaits on this sparkling night.
With chuckles and warmth to share and shout,
In this winter, it’s love that’s all about!

Enigmatic Gifts from the Frozen Sky

Under the snow, a funny surprise,
A rubber chicken in disguise.
Wrapped in frost with a bright red bow,
Winter's humor, stealing the show.

A penguin wearing a silly hat,
Slips on ice with a clumsy spat.
Laughter fills the chilly air,
While snowflakes tumble without a care.

Jolly snowmen dance with glee,
Mittens stolen by a squirrel, you see.
Chortles echo, hearts feel light,
As we revel in the frosty night.

A snowball fight with a great big grin,
Each throw a chance for laughter to win.
Behind every flake, a jest lies in wait,
Winter's punchline is never late.

Glimmering Memories Wrapped in Ice

A gift box spins upon the ground,
With silly socks, where fun is found.
Frosty hacks and giggles abound,
Laughter dances all around.

Shiny baubles on a tree,
Rattling like a bad symphony.
A cat jumps up, knocks it down,
Nice decorations turned to frown.

Candy canes in funny shapes,
Mishaps lead to great escapes.
The coffee spills, whoops, what a mess,
Winter’s charm is pure, no less.

Snowflakes shower down like jokes,
A world transformed into silly hoax.
Wrapped in warmth and comic cheer,
These frosty days are oh so dear.

Charmed Lights in the Frosty Realm

Twinkling lights, a sight that’s vivacious,
Singing carols, quite audacious.
A reindeer jumps, then trips on a wire,
In the frosty air, our laughter’s desire.

Snow flurries bring a playful tease,
As snowmen wobble in the breeze.
With carrot noses all askew,
Winter’s pranks, there’s always a few.

Surprises wrapped in shiny foil,
A winter party that's sure to spoil.
Dancing wildly, the cocoa spills,
Frosty fun gives us all the thrills.

Charming sights under the moon,
Funny hats make us sing a tune.
In this frosty realm of pure delight,
Every moment is a joke in the night.

Enchanted Breezes through the Winter Woods

Whispers float through icy pines,
Tickling noses and funny signs.
A squirrel dances a wacky jig,
While down below, a snowball digs.

The wind plays tricks with our hats,
Chasing them off, oh what of that?
Slipping and sliding on the ground,
Winter’s humor truly knows no bounds.

Frosty breath makes clouds of cheer,
With frozen giggles from ear to ear.
Snowflakes swirl in a curious dance,
Dreams of snowmen in a snowy trance.

Every turn brings a new surprise,
In this frosty world, we roam and rise.
Laughter echoes through the woods,
Winter's magic in merry hoods.

Cold Light Dancing on Snowy Fields

Snowflakes twirl like disco balls,
As penguins slide and make their calls.
Frosty breath in the chilly air,
While squirrels chatter without a care.

Jolly snowmen wear carrot hats,
While field mice jive with jazzy spats.
Snowball fights break out with glee,
As winter's fun is plain to see.

A reindeer slips upon the ice,
And giggles follow, oh so nice!
With all this fun, who needs the sun?
In snowy fields, we laugh and run.

Snow is here; let’s have a ball!
Who knew winter could be so tall?
With frosty jokes and cheerful cheer,
We'll make memories throughout the year.

Enchanted Wonders of the Frigid Realm

Jack Frost paints every window bright,
While penguins waltz in pure delight.
Icicles hang like jewels of glass,
As snowmen giggle with a sass.

Through snow-draped woods we prance and play,
Wishing on snowflakes, it’s a perfect day.
Elves in capes on candy canes,
Dance around while giggling trains.

Hot cocoa spills, oh what a fuss,
As puppy paws leave tracks with us.
Evergreens wear their frosty crowns,
And neighbors wear their silliest frowns.

In this realm of chilly fun,
Who knew frost could be so run?
With holiday tunes and laughter clear,
We toast to winter, give a cheer!

Frosted Echoes of the Milky Way

Stars twinkle bright on this chilly night,
Snowflakes sing and take their flight.
Cats in sweaters prance with glee,
As winter dances so playfully.

Around the fire with marshmallows toasted,
We laugh out loud, our worries roasted.
Frosty fingers and cozy smiles,
Laughter echoing for miles and miles.

Hot drinks spill on our woolly socks,
While playful snowmen toss their rocks.
Sledding down the hills we glide,
As snowball fights become our pride.

In the silence, there’s a cheer,
Winter's magic draws us near.
With starry nights and snowflakes sway,
Let’s crank up the fun in every way!

Chilling Delights and Radiant Sights

Chill in the air, but laughter abounds,
As children explore, jumping off mounds.
Frosty noses and rosy cheeks,
With silly hats that look like peaks.

Winter nights are icy and bright,
As snowmen dance beneath the light.
Ice skaters slip, bring giggles galore,
As a snowball strikes, “Not me!” we implore.

Glistening paths with a twinkling sheen,
While critters join in the winter scene.
Sleds on hills, a wild adventure,
Who knew winter could be such a denture?

In frosty bliss, we bundle tight,
With friends and laughter in the night.
Oh what jests the cold might bring,
Turning winter into a cheerful fling!

Luminous Offerings in Cold Embrace

A snowman wearing flip-flops,
Waves to children on the block.
His carrot nose has frozen glops,
While penguins dance around the clock.

The trees are dressed in glitter bright,
With squirrels sleighing on a whim.
Hot cocoa spills, a crazy sight,
As marshmallows all do swim.

A winter hat that's far too big,
On Grandpa's head, it slips and slides.
He trips and does a wobbly jig,
As laughter through the cold confides.

So here we cheer, with snowflakes falling,
And giggles loud in the crisp air.
With joy and laughter, they are calling,
These frosty days are beyond compare.

Whispers of Icicles and Dreams

A sneaky squirrel stole my mitt,
He wears it like a superhero.
Does he think he's fit for it?
Or just wants to steal the show?

Icicles hang like little swords,
Ready for a snowball fight.
Yet, rooftops drone with chilly chords,
As ice chips clink in pure delight.

Frosted windows paint our fate,
With scenes of scenes quite absurd.
I spotted Auntie on a plate,
A pie that jiggles, how absurd!

We gather close, as fires crack,
To tell of slips and falls outside.
Each winter tale hard to hold back,
While giggles twirl like snowflakes glide.

Radiant Treasures Beneath the Chill

Down the path, there’s a sledding race,
But wait—was that a turtle too?
Slow and steady takes first place,
As winter winds play peek-a-boo.

A treasure hunt for fluff and fluff,
With friends, each one will seek a prize.
A hidden snowball? That’s just rough!
And oh! That snowman’s sad surprise.

Buried deep beneath the snow,
A stash of socks that lost a mate.
We’ll save them all, just in case,
When winter’s warmth we can await.

With giggles bright, we carry on,
Through frosty fields and icy fun.
We laugh until the dew is gone,
While chasing rays of wintry sun.

Echoes of Frosted Serenades

The carolers are out of tune,
They harmonize with frozen feet.
A cat joins in, thinks it's a boon,
While snowflakes dance to the upbeat.

Pine cones decorate a chubby cat,
A festive hat made out of cheese.
She prances proud, and that is that,
As children giggle with such ease.

Snowballs fly with crazy aim,
But one lands right upon my head.
I laugh and shout that snow is game,
While icy winds are mischief-bred.

As night falls, lights flicker bold,
We share the stories, old and new.
With every laugh, warm hearts unfold,
This winter's charm, so bright and true.

Moonlit Miracles on the Frozen Lake

Under the moon, a squirrel slips,
Wearing a hat that fits his tips.
He slides and giggles, a frozen spree,
Laughing at fish who swim with glee.

A penguin waltzes, twirls with flair,
Wearing a scarf and a baffled stare.
He thinks he’s cool, but truth be told,
His dance is quite warm... a sight to behold!

Snowmen build dreams, hats piled high,
Using old cans for a twinkling eye.
But when they trip on their carrot nose,
They roll and tumble, with laughter arose!

The lake, it sparkles, a frosty show,
With critters dancing, stealing the glow.
While winter whispers, in chuckles and quirks,
The garden of mischief that nature works!

Glinting Reflections in the Quietest Hours

In the stillness, a cat on patrol,
Wearing long boots, trying to stroll.
He slides on ice, with a panicked meow,
Chasing his tail, a circus wow!

Snowflakes chuckle as sleds take flight,
Kids zoom by, shouting with delight.
But a rogue snowball, from out of the blue,
Turns the fun into a frosty goo!

Bunnies hop in their winter gear,
With hats too big, they shuffle near.
Each bounce they make sends snow flying,
And all around, the owls are sighing.

The stars twinkle, giving a wink,
As cocoa spills—oh, what a stink!
Yet laughter rings through the chilly night,
In winter's fun, all feels just right!

Shimmering Flurries in a Starlit Dance

A snowflake parade begins tonight,
With dancers dressed in purest white.
They shimmy and shake, with glitter galore,
While snowshoes get stuck, what a chore!

Crisp air fills lungs, a laugh escapes,
A moose in mittens, with throaty shapes.
He slips on ice, as onlookers cheer,
Waving his arms, 'I'm a prince, oh dear!'

The stars above play peek-a-boo,
Annoyed at the moon, for stealing their cue.
But in such gleeful chaos, they twinkle bright,
Adding to the charm of this merry night!

A fox with a broom sweeps the snow,
While critters gather, putting on a show.
With each twirl and flip, joy intertwines,
In shimmering flurries, the humor shines!

Echoes of Warmth in the Winter's Glow

The fireplace crackles, hot cocoa's near,
While marshmallows dive into mugs with cheer.
A bear in pajamas stirs the pot,
Wants spicy marshmallows—oh, why not?

Chickadees chirp in their lovely coats,
Complaining about how winter gloats.
With beaks full of seeds and laughter, they sing,
About the joy that the cold can bring.

Icicles dangle with a gleaming threat,
While squirrels plan pranks, as of yet unmet.
The mischief they plot, oh, what a thrill,
With winter's laughter, they've got time to kill!

As laughter echoes through frosty air,
With joy and warmth, it's a winter affair.
In cozy corners, hearts dance and sway,
Creating memories that brighten the gray!

Shining Echoes Within the Winter's Breath

Oh look, a snowman with a hat,
He waves his stick, and then he sat.
His eyes are buttons, slightly askew,
Is he smiling, or just feeling blue?

The sleigh bells jingle, but it’s just me,
Chasing my dog who’s lost in a tree.
He thinks it's fun, I declare it chaos,
His tail a blur, my patience a loss.

A snowball fight with mom and dad,
Laughter erupts, the chaos is rad.
But someone slipped, oh what a sight,
Now dad’s a snow angel, oh what a fright!

Hot cocoa spills on my new scarf,
Guess I’m just a walking art-parf.
Yet with each laugh and frozen cheer,
Winter’s mischief brings us all near.

Luminous Traces of Frosted Dawn

The icicles dangle, a sugar-bent prize,
Mom's got her mittens, and oh how she cries!
'You kids keep playing in the frostbite!'
But we're making snow angels, what a light!

The cats on the roof think they're in a show,
Like feline acrobats, they're putting on glow.
They leap and they land with a great little thump,
And I giggle, then face-plant in a snowy lump!

We deck the halls with lights that blink,
While dad tries to untangle around his drink.
He wraps the tree, then takes a nap,
Dreaming of sledding with Santa and a map.

And when the night falls, dogs start to howl,
At the glow of the moon and the sneaky old owl.
We all sit together, the world wrapped in white,
Sharing the stories that warm up the night.

Tales Carved in Crystal Silence

In a forest of pine, a squirrel takes flight,
Dodging the snowflakes, oh what a sight!
His treasure is acorns, he hoards with glee,
But loses his stash, what a sight to see!

A rabbit hops near, with a twitch of a nose,
Hoping for carrots, maybe a rose.
He digs through the snow and finds just a sock,
Fashion statement or snack? He takes stock!

The children venture, they build and they clash,
Snow forts arise, while snowballs go splash.
Their laughter erupts as they tumble and roll,
Winter's circus, losing all self-control!

With cocoa in hand and a warm little cheer,
We trade our tales with a kid-friendly jeer.
For glittery moments wrapped in the cold,
Lay the best stories ever told.

Twinkling Hues of Seasonal Shimmer

Now the lights are all strung, what a jolly sight,
Mom bumbles around, giving everyone fright.
She’s tangled in ribbons, oh what a mess,
We just cheer her on, with joy and finesse!

The cookies are burnt, but the kids don’t mind,
‘They’re extra crunchy!’ They say, feeling blind.
We scoop up the sprinkles with glee in our hearts,
Shouts fill the air as the fun never departs.

The old dog snoozes by the fire’s warm glare,
He dreams of sneaking snacks, not a single care.
With paws all a-wiggle, his snores fill the room,
Winter is silly; it banishes gloom!

As the night deepens and tales start to weave,
We laugh about snowflakes that dare to deceive.
These moments so silly, wrapped tight like a bow,
Are the gifts that we cherish, soft as the snow.

The Lullaby of Icicles Hanging

Icicles dangle with a playful sway,
Dropping droplets on my head today.
The sun shines bright, melting a bit,
With each little plop, I dodge and split.

Snowflakes dance on rooftops high,
Each one whispers a snowy sigh.
I laugh at the chill, my nose goes red,
Sipping hot cocoa, a treat instead.

Frosty friends in hats and scarves,
Join in antics, they make me laugh.
With snowmen boasting, 'Look at me!'
I chuckle at their frosty glee.

So here's to winter, a jolly sight,
Filled with mischief and pure delight.
Icicles laugh as they fall and freeze,
A chorus of joy in the winter breeze.

Wishes Carried by the Winter Wind

A big round moon sits up so high,
Wishes ride on puffs that fly.
With laughter swirling in the air,
I toss my dreams without a care.

The wind collects them, playful tease,
Sending them dancing through the trees.
I chase after them, slipping and sliding,
As snowmen giggle, gleefully priding.

Frosty whispers tease my ear,
'Not all your wishes will come near.'
Yet here I stand with dreams so bright,
Laughing with joy, what a silly sight!

Through flurries, I waddle with grace,
Chasing my hopes in this winter place.
Each puff a chuckle, a frosty grin,
Merry and bright, let the fun begin!

Lanterns of Hope in the Cold

Lanterns glow, flickering light,
Guiding the way through the chilly night.
They laugh and giggle, a jolly cheer,
Casting shadows full of winter's weird!

A parade of lights on a frosty lane,
I stumble past snowdrifts, isn't it a pain?
Yet twinkling laughter fills the air,
As I slip on ice, busting my affair.

With every step, I spread some cheer,
While snowflakes stick to my nose, oh dear!
The lanterns wink, they seem to say,
'Get up, don't pout, it's all just play!'

So dance with me in this sparkling glow,
Turning shivers into a joyful show.
Wrapped in warmth, we laugh out loud,
In this winter wonderland, oh how proud!

Reflections on a Frost-Kissed Pond

A pond like glass, so neat and fine,
Mirrors the trees like a silly design.
I skitter and slide, trying to find,
My balance, oh dear, I'm quite behind!

Frog princes croak in a goofy tune,
As I whirl and twirl under the moon.
Their jumps make me giggle, what a sight,
I join the dance, feeling so light.

Silly old ducks paddle in place,
Quacking together with comical grace.
I wave and they quack, it's a merry sound,
Winter's a party, joy all around.

Reflections ripple with laughter and cheer,
A chill in the air, but warmth is near.
With each frozen step, my heart takes flight,
Embracing the fun in this frosty night!

Dazzling Shades in the Quiet Frost

The snowflakes dance in silly spins,
The squirrels wearing tiny grins.
A snowman’s carrot nose is quite askew,
He thought he'd look cool if he wore one too.

The icicles hang like teeth of steel,
Don't get too close or you might feel!
The frozen pond calls kids for a slide,
But don’t forget to bounce on the other side!

In jackets too big, they waddle with glee,
Looking like marshmallows, can't you see?
The hot cocoa steams, but spills on the floor,
While laughter erupts from the cupboard door!

Through the frosty air, a snowball flies,
Just like a comet, bright in the skies!
The winter may chill, but hearts stay warm,
In this silly season, there's always charm!

Celestial Gifts of the Silent Season

Pine trees wear sweaters, oh what a sight,
Shimmery ornaments spark with delight.
The ornaments wobble on branches so high,
While cats launch a strike, giving presents a try!

A reindeer's antlers get stuck in the snow,
He shakes them off fast, 'I'm ready to go!'
Frosty cheeks turn a rosy hue,
As kids throw snowballs higher than you!

Chimneys puff smoke like they're sneezing,
Hot cocoa spills as they're all just wheezing.
The elves on the shelf hold up their sides,
While Santa's sleigh slides and giggles collide.

On quiet nights, the snowflakes cheer,
"Come join the fun, spread joy, never fear!"
With cheerful shouts echoing around,
In this humorous time, laughter is found!

Whispered Tranquility of Frosty Evenings

The moonlight shines on snowflakes bright,
As creatures play hide and seek through the night.
Penguins in pajamas slide on the ground,
Taking silly tumbles, round and round!

A snow angel waves, covered in frost,
While kids build igloos and get completely lost.
The twinkling stars giggle and tease,
As mittens fall off and float in the breeze.

The cats chase shadows, making quite the fuss,
While hot pies cool with nibbles from us.
Frosty the snowman tries to sing,
But only sounds like a tuba's zing!

In cozy homes, laughter abounds,
With tales of winter and silly sounds.
This tranquil night hides giggles galore,
As frosty dreams knock softly at the door!

Serendipitous Shimmers Beneath the Moon

Underneath the moon, the snowflakes sway,
Like dancers having the time of their day.
A snowball fight breaks out in a flash,
While puppy joins in with a happy dash!

The stars wink down on snowy attire,
As mittens and hats start to catch fire.
Jokes slip and slide in the chilly chill,
As laughter erupts, giving hearts a thrill!

Icicles dangle with comedic flair,
As squirrels prepare for their prank-filled air.
A flurry of snow makes it hard to see,
Yet laughter erupts, as all agree.

In the quiet moments, giggles do bloom,
As hot chocolate spills all over the room!
With cozy blankets and stories to share,
This winter evening is beyond compare!

Enchanted Reflections on Icy Waters

A penguin slipped with quite a flair,
He danced around in chilly air.
With flippers wide, he took a glide,
The fish all laughed, they tried to hide.

Snowflakes fell like little clowns,
Tickling noses, making frowns.
The frostbite took a playful bite,
And all the snowmen started to fight.

A moose adorned with twinkling lights,
Pranced around in snowy fights.
I tried to catch him, what a sport,
But he just giggled and ran short!

In the mirror-like ice so bright,
We laughed until we felt the bite.
With every slip, a joyful cheer,
Oh, winter's fun, we hold so dear!

Secret Treasures Beneath the Snow

Under blankets of white fluff,
Lurk secret snacks and treats quite tough.
A squirrel dug with great delight,
For acorns hidden out of sight.

Snowmen stash some festive cake,
With frosting on their heads they ache.
A carrot nose tries to deceive,
But melted eyes start to believe.

A rabbit missed the winter stew,
He wore a hat, oh such a view!
With fluffy ears all crisp and snug,
He wiggled around just like a bug.

So when the snow begins to fall,
Remember all, we've gifts for all.
The treasure's not the gold or fame,
But laughter shared, our winter game!

Aurora's Gift in the Stillness

The lights danced bright, a quirky show,
With colors that giggled like a pro.
The moose wore shades and looked quite fab,
As northern lights turned drab to lab.

In the stillness, a fox did prance,
Chasing shadows, lost in trance.
He tripped and tumbled in the fray,
Then blinked and said, "What a fine day!"

With a wink, the stars began to tease,
A deer tried dancing with such ease.
But then he slipped and fell with grace,
Leaving snowflakes all on his face.

So as we watch this cosmic play,
Let’s join the fun, hip-hip-hooray!
For winter’s charm is full of jest,
A time for laughter, we’re truly blessed!

Twinkling Stars on a Frosty Night

The stars above begin to wink,
While snowmen toast their cocoa drink.
A polar bear joined in the fun,
He cracked a joke, oh what a pun!

With every twinkle, a giggle flows,
As Santa's sleigh hitched up the bows.
Reindeer laughed till they ran amok,
Until they slipped on frosty rock.

A snowball fight broke out with cheer,
The snowflakes whispered, "Get him here!"
With giggles ringing through the night,
Their frosty bites were quite the sight.

So gather 'round and share a laugh,
With winter's joy, we'll take a bath.
In twinkling stars and snowy flight,
We celebrate this frosty night!

Crystalline Moments in Nature's Silence

In frosty air, a snowman grins,
His carrot nose, where humor spins.
With button eyes that wink and blink,
He's plotting how to steal my drink.

The icicles dangle like pointy hats,
While squirrels debate the best of chats.
One jumps high, the other takes flight,
Both fail to land, what a silly sight!

A snowball fight ensues with glee,
But I missed my mark, got hit by a tree.
Laughter rings out, oh what a show,
In winter’s grip, we steal the glow.

As flakes fall down like fluffy seeds,
The kids make angels, fulfilling their needs.
Yet I trip once more, on my own two feet,
Landing headfirst where joy and snow meet.

Frigid Sentiments Wrapped in Light

The twinkling lights on branches sway,
Each bulb shines bright like a clown's bouquet.
I stumble in the dance of frost,
In my own story, I've totally lost!

Hot cocoa spills as I wave hello,
A marshmallow lands on my cheek, oh no!
The laughter erupts, cups raised high,
Cheers to the mess, oh me, oh my!

With mittens tight, I take my aim,
But throw a snowball that's utterly lame.
It hits my friend with a soft little plop,
"Is that your best?" oh, I can't stop!

Plans for the snow fort are made with glee,
But it collapses on top of me.
Buried in snow, I'm the sight of the day,
Call me the ice queen, come what may!

Wonders of a Frosty Dreamscape

In a land where snowflakes giggle and dance,
A frosty deer gave winter a glance.
Wearing a scarf, he strutted with flair,
Chasing his tail without a care!

The rabbits have parties, or so I've heard,
They sing and they dance, not a single word.
Though one jumps high and lands on a pie,
"Well, that's one way to eat," I sigh!

Snowmen gossip by the old oak tree,
Trading tall tales about the winter spree.
"Did you see the giant that came by last night?
He took my nose, what a silly fright!"

As icicles drip like the best of tricks,
Chasing each other, we perform silly kicks.
With winter's laughs wrapped in a snowy embrace,
We dance through the chill, at our own crazy pace.

Dazzling Solitude Beneath the Snow

A snowflake lands right on my nose,
Tickling softly, like a friend who knows.
“I’m here to tell you winter’s a go!”
“Thanks for the warning!” I laugh in the glow.

With penguin socks, I shuffle along,
My grumpy cat watches, he thinks it’s wrong.
Every step's a dance, a slip, then a spin,
Watching my pets, who think they can win.

The trees wear coats made of fluffy white,
Whispering secrets about the night’s delight.
But I trip to the left, and whoops, down I fall,
Rolling like snowball, I giggle through it all!

And so we roam through shimmering skies,
With comical slips beneath our blue sighs.
Each moment a gift, wrapped up in moonlight,
We laugh till it hurts, oh what a delight!

Treasures Wrapped in Winter's Breath

Snowflakes dance like tipsy sprites,
In hats that fit just a bit too tight.
Ornaments on trees start to sing,
While neighbors argue about the best bling.

Pine cones wear their seasonal best,
With squirrels prepping for a nutty fest.
Chilly winds take playful jabs,
At plump carolers with frosty drabs.

Cookies tiptoe on icy floors,
While reindeer snack on doorknob tours.
Frosty breath brings giggles near,
As Santa hops with a grin and cheer.

Hot cocoa spills on woolly gloves,
As laughter wraps us in cozy hugs.
Under twinkling lights we jive and sway,
In this chilly, chuckling holiday play.

Silvered Leaves Under a Pale Moon

Crystals sparkle in moonlit frost,
Each step I take, I feel like a boss.
Raccoons in tuxedos throw a ball,
While snowmen try to stand up tall.

A carrot's nose starts to wiggle,
As frosty winds make it giggle.
Trees hang ornaments that never end,
As snowy owls decide to blend.

Marshmallows leap from mugs with glee,
While gingerbread men play hide and see.
In the stillness, giggles erupt,
As snowflakes find their way to interrupt.

Icicles act like nature's teeth,
As polar bears dance under a wreath.
With each chilly breath, we share delight,
In this winter wonderland, all feels right.

Dreamscapes of the Frozen World

In the land of ice with frosty cheer,
Penguins in bow ties slide without fear.
Marshmallow clouds float in the blue,
As snowglobes wink at me and you.

Sleds zoom by like rockets in flight,
While snowflakes race, oh what a sight!
Icicles hang like Christmas lights,
With raccoons planning mischievous nights.

Chubby snowmen don’t stand a chance,
When the wind starts up a frosty dance.
Hot chocolate spills as we laugh and cheer,
With snowballs flying far and near.

Dreams of winter make spirits bright,
As nature snickers in pure delight.
The frozen world is our playful stage,
With every chuckle, we turn the page.

Joyous Lights in the Depth of December

Twinkling bulbs like stars on parade,
As snowflakes play tag and invade.
Dancing snowmen lose their hats,
While reindeer munch on dinner chats.

Hot pies cooling on the window ledge,
Make cats pounce and take the edge.
Mittens lost in a snowy spree,
As kids build forts beneath the trees.

Socks with holes become the style,
As we chuckle and share a smile.
Light shows blink like stars on speed,
While frosty fingers fumble, indeed.

In December's heart, we find our way,
With laughter and love and a sprinkle of play.
Through joyous lights, the world is spun,
In a whimsical dance that's just begun.

Hushed Murmurs of the Winter Breeze

The snowflakes dance like silly sprites,
They tickle noses, give little bites.
Each gust of wind, a gentle tease,
Makes us laugh with icy ease.

In scarves so thick, we waddle by,
Look like penguins who can't fly.
With boots that slip, we twist and turn,
Our winter waltz is quite the learn.

Hot cocoa spills, a creamy splash,
As marshmallows bounce in a fluffy crash.
Sipping slow, a frosty must,
Laughter bubbles, warmth is just.

So come, dear friends, let's make a scene,
In winter's joke, we'll reign supreme.
With chilly giggles, and frosty fun,
We'll frolic until the day is done.

Radiance Amongst the Snowfall

The stars above all twinkle bright,
They're playing hide and seek tonight.
While snowflakes shimmer, soft and wide,
They dance like disco balls outside.

A boots-on-snow sound, a crunching song,
A snowman built, a little wrong.
With a carrot nose and eyes of coal,
He grins so wide, he's on a roll.

From frosty breaths, we chase our pride,
Like dragons puffing, we cannot hide.
But look, a slip, a tumble down,
We giggle loud, no need to frown.

So gather close, in the falling flake,
Let's make a mess for laughter's sake.
In winter's joy, we all can find,
A touch of whimsy, sweet and kind.

The Warmth of Flickering Hearthlight

The fire crackles, pops with glee,
A dancing face for all to see.
With marshmallows roasting, oh, what a sight,
They puff up big, and add delight.

We snuggle close, our faces aglow,
Discussing all the things we know.
From silly jokes to stories tall,
The warmth of laughter conquers all.

In cozy nooks, we sip our cheer,
Hot apple cider, winter's beer!
With giggles rising, spirits soar,
Our hearts aglow, who could ask for more?

So toast a cheer, for every friend,
In light and warmth, our laughs transcend.
With winter’s charm, we’ll never tire,
As long as there’s food and cozy fire!

Frosty Caresses of the Night Sky

The moon peeks down, a cheeky face,
In the night sky, he finds his place.
As snowflakes swirl, they shout with glee,
It’s a frosty party, just you and me.

Stars strut around in glittering shoes,
They twinkle and wink, sharing the news.
Come join the fun, we mustn’t wait,
For in this chill, we celebrate!

Snow angels spread their frosty wings,
While laughter erupts, oh the joy it brings.
With sleds and slides, we race and glide,
Oh what fun, in winter we ride!

So gather your mittens, bundle up tight,
Let’s take on this frosted, starry night.
With every flake, our spirits rise,
In a world of giggles beneath moonlit skies.

Frosted Tales of Timeless Beauty

In a snowman's hat, a squirrel's found,
He thinks he's the king, but he's just round.
Carrots for noses, we all laugh aloud,
As he shimmies and shakes, oh so proud.

Penguins on ice, doing the cha-cha,
Slipping and sliding, oh what a drama.
They strut their stuff in a frosty show,
Waddling around, just stolen the show.

Hot cocoa spills, marshmallows fly,
A snowball fight turns into a pie!
Mittens thrown like little bombs,
In this winter game, chaos calms.

Jingle bells ringing, but someone forgot,
To bring the cookies, oh what a plot!
We feast on snowflakes, sweetened just right,
In our frosted tales, the fun takes flight.

Radiance in the Heart of Winter

The penguin parade, oh what a sight,
Waddling in line, giving hugs tight.
With little bow ties and sparkly hats,
They dance in circles, just like acrobats.

A snowball's flung, it lands on a sleigh,
The reindeer laugh, 'I'll get you someday!'
With noses all red and scarves tied in knots,
They prance on rooftops, warming the spots.

Icicles dangle from the rooftops high,
Like frozen chandeliers, they twinkle and sigh.
But one little drip, oh where will it land?
Right on a snowman, oh isn't it grand?

We sip hot chocolate, giggles in the air,
With whipped cream mountains, a frosty flair.
In winter's embrace, joy's here on cue,
With laughter that sparkles like falling flakes too.

Luminescence in the Whispering Pines

Under the pines, a secret dance,
Where squirrels wear boots with a daring prance.
They twirl and they spin, round and around,
Even the snowflakes can't help but bounce.

Beneath the stars, a rabbit takes flight,
On a sled made of carrots, soaring the night.
With a wink and a hop, he steals all the show,
Shouting, 'Hold tight, I'm ready to go!'

The owls in the trees, give a wise little hoot,
As the skaters perform in their winter boot.
With marshmallows roasting, the night is so bright,
Under glow of moonbeams, it's pure delight.

Toasting chilly toes by the warmth of the fire,
With tales that will lift us, lift us much higher.
Laughter erupts with each goofy twirl,
Amidst frosted wonders, their magic unfurl.

Sacred Moments in the Radiant Snow

In a snow globe world, we jump and we spin,
With frosty confetti, let the fun begin.
We build a tall castle, so grand and so wide,
Only to watch it get stuck in the tide.

Rabbits in scarves, they hop in a race,
With carrots for trophies, they're setting the pace.
So quick on their feet, with giggles galore,
Each time they skid, we just want more!

The cat on the roof, with a frosty tail,
Watches the chaos, her patience on veil.
But round and round, the children play fast,
With laughter that echoes, a cheer unsurpassed.

We'll sip on hot cider, tell stories on cue,
Of snowmen who dance and of owls that flew.
These moments, though silly, are treasured with glee,
As we cherish winter's sweet jubilee.

Celestial Embrace in the Frosty Veil

Snowflakes dance and twirl about,
Making snowmen, look at them pout!
A carrot snatched, a hat askew,
They grumble 'Hey, we’re cold, it’s true!'

Frosty breath like dragons puff,
Neighbors laughing, isn’t it rough?
Sledding down the hill with a squeal,
Oops! Did someone lose their meal?

Hats and mittens, a mismatched sight,
Trying to see, but oh what a fright!
A snowball flies, the laughter rings,
Who knew winter would have such swings!

And as the moon gives a cheeky grin,
We toast to winter, let the fun begin!
With frostbitten noses and cheeks so red,
We’ll share our stories, then go to bed!

Luminescent Whispers Through the Pines

Through the trees, those twinkling lights,
Squirrels chirp in festive flights.
What's that? A choir of owls at play?
Or just the frost making them sway?

Decking out branches with flair and fun,
Who knew pines could dance in the sun?
The ornaments wobble, the ribbons tangle,
A holiday bash? Oh, what a jangle!

Snowdrifts hid gifts well and tight,
Jumping in piles, oh what a sight!
But finding a gift beneath a chilly mound,
Turns into falling and rolling around!

With cookies cooling, the scents arise,
But somehow our cat has her spies!
We play and laugh, what chaos, what cheer,
In this wild wonderland, we've nothing to fear!

Delicate Crystals Under the Moonlit Sky

Ice crystals twinkle like stars on the grass,
What's that noise? It's the dog chasing fast!
He slips and slides, what a comical sight,
Barking at shadows that give quite a fright!

Under the moon, we gather in cheer,
Sip cocoa spiked with a bit of beer.
Laughter erupts with each silly joke,
As we build a snow fort, not a piddling poke!

We toss snowballs with most excellent aim,
But wait, who's winning this ridiculous game?
With hairdos adorned in snowflakes and more,
Can anyone still tell whose hair's on the floor?

When the night ends with a twinkling bow,
We'll dream of the flurries that made us all glow.
With cheeks so rosy from laughter and fun,
We'll cherish these moments 'til springtime has sprung!

Silvery Reflections in the Glazed Landscape

The world wrapped in silver, a dazzling sight,
But kids on skates make it quite a fright!
With each little twirl and every big fall,
It's a comedy show, oh laughter for all!

The frozen pond, a shimmering stage,
Their clumsy prance sets the scene for a page.
A toasty fire, the hot dogs we roast,
Yet why did Uncle Joe ghost us the most?

Brrr! That getaway flask just might slip,
Spilling hot cider, a sugary drip.
It flows like a river, sticky and sweet,
We all end up laughing at the clumsy feat!

As stars pop out in a clap of delight,
We'll reminisce 'til the fall of the night.
With cheeks aflame and spirits so bright,
Who knew winter fun could reach such great height?